Rainforests

Anita Ganeri

First published 2011 by Kingfisher
This edition published 2013 by Kingfisher
an imprint of Macmillan Children's Books
a division of Macmillan Publishers Limited
20 New Wharf Road, London N1 9RR
Basingstoke and Oxford
Associated companies throughout the world
www.panmacmillan.com

Illustrations by: Peter Bull Art Studio

ISBN 978-0-7534-3659-2

1 3 5 7 9 8 6 4 2

1TR/0413/WKT/UNTD/128MA

A CIP catalogue record for this book is available from
the British Library.

Printed in China

Picture credits

**The Publisher would like to thank the following
for permission to reproduce their material.
(t = top, b = bottom, c = centre, l = left, r = right):**
Pages 4l Corbis/Wolfgang Kaehler; 4c Frank Lane Picture
Agency (FLPA)/Thomas Marent/Minden; 5tl Corbis/David Aubry;
5tr FLPA/Mark Moffett/Minden; 5cl Shutterstock/dean bertoncelj;
5br PA/Andy Wong/AP; 6bl Photolibrary/Robert Harding; 8cl
Photolibrary/Kitch Bain; 8tr Ardea/Thomas Marent; 9tl Alamy/
AfriPics.com; 9tr Ardea/Nick Gordon; 9cr Shutterstock/Dr Morley
Read; 9bl Photolibrary/OSF; 9br Naturepl/James Aldred; 10tl
Shutterstock/Peter Leahy; 12cl FLPA/Imagebroker; 12bl
Photolibrary/OSF; 12-13 Naturepl/Pete Oxford; 13tr FLPA/
Patricia & Michael Fogden /Minden; 13bc Photolibrary/OSF;
13br FLPA/Thomas Marent/Minden; 14bl FLPA/Patricia & Michael
Fogden /Minden; 16l Shutterstock/Jean-Edouard Rozey; 16r
Shutterstock/javarman; 17tl Photolibrary/Chua Wee Boo; 17cr
FLPA/Frans Lanting; 17bl FLPA/Patricia & Michael Fogden/
Minden; 17br FLPA/Piotr Nasrecki; 18bl FLPA/SA Team/Minden;
20tl FLPA/Imagebroker; 20cl Photolibrary/digital vision; 20c FLPA
/Thomas Marent/Minden; 20-21t Photolibrary/Robert Harding; 21cl
FLPA/Tim Fitzharris/Minden; 21tr Shutterstock/Janne Hamalainen;
21br FLPA/Tui De Roy/Minden; 21bc Photolibary/All Canada
Photos; 22tl Photolibrary/Wave RF; 24cl Alamy/blickwinkel; 24b
Naturepl/Martin Dohrn; 25tl Photolibrary/Tips Italia; 25cl Alamy/
Edward Parker; 25cr Corbis/Wendy Stone; 25bc Alamy/
BrazilPhotos.com; 26tl Shutterstock/Vladimir Wrangel; 28l Corbis/
Stephanie Maze; 28cr FLPA/Claus Meyer; 28br Corbis/Yusef
Ahmad; 29tl Alamy/Wildlife GmbH; 29tc FLPA/Cyril Ruoso/
Minden; 29cr Alamy/Bon Appetit; 29b Reuters/Enrique Castro-
Mendivil; 30tl Shutterstock/dean bertoncelj; 30ctl Alamy/Danita
Delimont; 30ctr Naturepl/Pete Oxford; 30bl Alamy/Anyka; 30br
FLPA/Reinhard Dirschel; 31tl Corbis/Mark Karrass; 31tr Alamy/
Robert Harding; 31ctl Shutterstock/Dr Morely Read; 31bl FLPA/
Tui De Roy/Minden; 31br Corbis/Nik Wheeler.

Contents

More to explore

On some of the pages in this book, you will find coloured buttons with symbols on them. There are four different colours, and each belongs to a different topic. Choose a topic, follow its coloured buttons through the book, and you'll make some interesting discoveries of your own.

For example, on page 7 you'll find a green button, like this, next to some orchids. The green buttons are about plants.

Page 15

Plants

There is a page number in the button. Turn to that page (page 15) to find a green button next to more plants: some tree roots. Follow all the steps through the book, and at the end of your journey you'll find out how the steps are linked, and discover even more information about this topic.

World

Environment

Minibeasts

The other topics in this book are world, environment and minibeasts. Follow the steps and see what you can discover!

Around the world

Rainforests grow along the Equator where it is hot, wet and steamy all year round. Although they only cover about a sixth of the Earth, they are home to millions of different plants and animals – more than any other habitat.

The roots of rainforest trees form a tangle on the gloomy forest floor. Above them, the trees grow to different heights, with the very tallest poking out into the sunshine.

A baby orang-utan shelters from the rain under a leaf.

tree frog,
South America

Scientists investigate the world's rainforests and, every year, they make exciting discoveries. For example, they find new plants that could be used as medicines.

A scientist on safety ropes studies a rainforest tree high above the ground.

Animals find plenty of food to eat among the rainforest trees. About half of all the world's known species of animals live in rainforests.

People have lived in rainforests for thousands of years. The forest gives them everything they need. But today, rainforests are being cut down and rainforest people are losing their homes.

Thousands of kinds of orchids live in the world's rainforests.

Penan people, southeast Asia

Rain falls nearly every day in the rainforest. There are often thunderstorms in the afternoon. The rain waters all the plants.

Towering trees

Poking out above the rainforest is a scattering of giant trees, called emergents. Some are an incredible 60m tall – as high as a 20-storey building. They are battered by howling winds and often struck by lightning.

Page 14

What is this?

① Colugos live off leaves, shoots, flowers and fruit.

② a tangle of lianas (woody vines)

③ Orchids grow along the mossy branches.

? These are an eagle's claw-like talons. The eagle uses its talons to snatch animals to eat.

4

5

Page 22

Page 15

6

High above a rainforest in southeast Asia, the tree branches are draped in lianas and orchids. A colugo glides between the trees. Its legs are joined by folds of furry skin which it uses like wings. Close behind, an enormous golden eagle comes swooping down. It needs food for the hungry chicks waiting in its nest.

4 A Philippine golden eagle soars through the air.

5 The dipterocarp is one of the tallest emergent trees.

6 Eagle chicks wait in their nest of sticks.

Parrots, such as these colourful conures, live in noisy flocks high up in the trees. They use their strong, curved beaks to feed on fruits, seeds, flower buds and insects.

A spider monkey can swing from a branch by its tail.

Spider monkeys spend their lives in the treetops and are expert climbers. They use their spidery arms, legs and tails to grip on to the branches.

black-handed spider monkey, Central America

conures, South America

In the treetops

Many animals and plants live in the emergent layer – or spend time there. Different species are found in different rainforests around the world. Wherever they live, they all have to cope with the strong winds and high temperatures in their treetop habitats.

The pink flowers of couratari trees add colour to the forest. After flowering, the trees grow fruit, then seeds with little 'wings' that are blown away by the wind.

Couratari trees grow in the rainforests of South America. Some are as tall as 50m.

Red colobus monkeys have furry coats, with a red back, white tummy and black arms and face. They live in large groups and spend most of their time high up in the treetops, feeding on leaves and fruit.

red colubus monkey, Africa

A scientist climbing a tualang tree needs a good head for heights. Tualangs grow in southeast Asia and are among the world's tallest trees, reaching 90m in height.

Page 18

What is this?

1. A toucan reaches for some juicy fruit.
2. A three-toed sloth clings to a branch.
3. The emerald tree boa is a superb climber.

Crowded canopy

Beneath the emergent trees, a thick, green roof of leaves grows over the rainforest. This roof is called the canopy. Bursting with life and colour, it is home to two-thirds of the forest's plants and animals, from tiny insects and creepy-crawlies, to snakes, birds and monkeys.

4 Red-flowered bromeliads grow on the branches.

5 The scarlet macaw is a kind of parrot.

6 A howler monkey spots the snake and sounds the alarm.

Page 19

Page 22

This tangle of branches and vines is the canopy of the Amazon rainforest. Hanging upside-down from a branch is a sleepy sloth with her baby clinging to her fur. Colourful toucans and macaws search for fruit among the trees. Meanwhile, howler monkeys warn off intruders with ear-splitting shrieks.

This is a close-up of the shimmering pattern on a morpho butterfly's wing.

Life in the canopy

The canopy gets plenty of sunshine and rain, so it is always warm and wet. These are ideal conditions for plants to grow in. In turn, the plants provide food and shelter for hundreds of canopy creatures.

Tarsiers have huge eyes for seeing in the dark.

Leafcutter ants are incredibly strong. An ant can carry a piece of leaf 50 times heavier than itself. The ants snip off leaves with their jaws and carry them back to their nests.

Parson's chameleon, Africa

The ants use their leaves as gardens to grow fungus to eat.

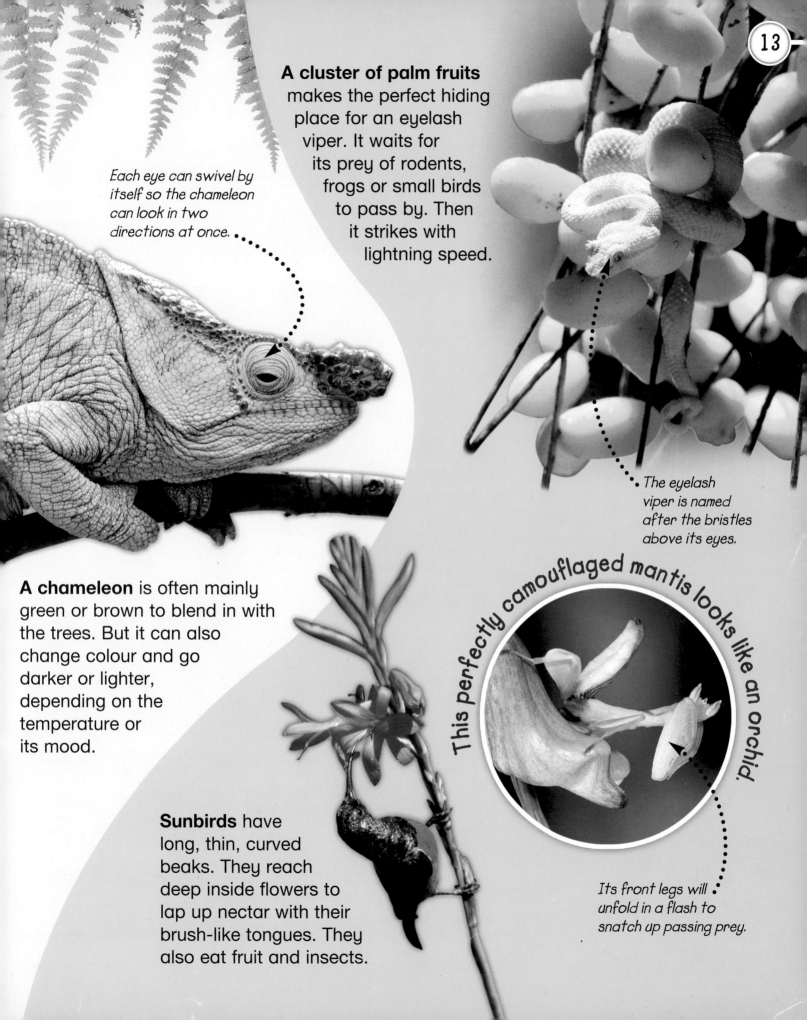

Each eye can swivel by itself so the chameleon can look in two directions at once.

A cluster of palm fruits makes the perfect hiding place for an eyelash viper. It waits for its prey of rodents, frogs or small birds to pass by. Then it strikes with lightning speed.

The eyelash viper is named after the bristles above its eyes.

A chameleon is often mainly green or brown to blend in with the trees. But it can also change colour and go darker or lighter, depending on the temperature or its mood.

This perfectly camouflaged mantis looks like an orchid.

Its front legs will unfold in a flash to snatch up passing prey.

Sunbirds have long, thin, curved beaks. They reach deep inside flowers to lap up nectar with their brush-like tongues. They also eat fruit and insects.

On the forest floor

Way down on the rainforest floor, it is always dark and gloomy. Only the odd shaft of sunlight ever reaches here. A maze of roots and rotting leaves covers the ground. The air smells stale and musty – there is very little breeze.

Page 11

What is this?

1 A pair of jewel beetles shimmer on a leaf.

2 a shy and solitary okapi

3 The record-breaking goliath frog is up to 30cm long.

? This is a close-up of the markings on a gaboon viper's head.

Despite the darkness, the floor of this rainforest in Africa is a busy place. Driver ants on the march swarm along a fallen tree trunk. Cunningly camouflaged against the leaf litter, a deadly gaboon viper is about to strike. An assassin bug has already caught its insect prey and is beginning to suck out its victim's insides.

Page 26

Page 30

4 A forest elephant forages for leaves and fruit.

5 Royal antelopes are about the size of rabbits – just 25cm tall!

6 An assassin bug attacks an African driver ant.

Life in the shade

Forest floor creatures have special features to help them survive. Many rely on camouflage to avoid being seen. Some have colours and patterns that blend in perfectly with fallen leaves. Others are hidden by the dapples of light and shade.

large, bony crest for display

A cassowary is a large, colourful bird. It cannot fly but it can run very fast. The cassowary feeds on fruit that has fallen to the forest floor. It swallows the fruit whole.

cassowary, New Guinea and Australia

A tiger gets close to its victim, then pounces.

A Sumatran tiger prowls through the undergrowth. Its stripy coat helps to hide it among the dapples of sunlight as it stalks its prey.

Rafflesia flowers look and smell like rotten meat. The terrible smell attracts flies and beetles which visit the flowers and pollinate them. Pollinating means carrying pollen from flower to flower so that seeds and new flowers can grow.

The rafflesia can measure 3m across and is the world's largest flower.

long, bendy snout for foraging on fruit and seeds

Tapirs are shy, secretive creatures that are mostly active at night. They live in Central and South America, following well-worn paths through the forest. They like to live close to water and are good swimmers.

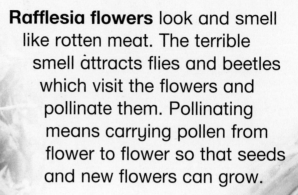

A bushmaster snake looks like a pile of leaves on the forest floor.

A dead-leaf katydid has wings that look exactly like dead leaves. When it sits perfectly still on the forest floor, the insect is impossible to see. This helps to hide it from enemies.

dead-leaf katydid, South America

Rainforest river

Rivers and streams flow across the forest floor.
Animals come here to feed and drink, in the water
and among the thick plants along the banks.
But life can be dangerous. Heavy rains can
make rivers flood, putting animals at risk.

1

Page 15

Page 30

6

What is this?

?

5

1 a fishing bat
swooping low

2 a capybara family
on the riverbank

3 a green
anaconda

? These are a piranha's razor-sharp teeth, which can strip flesh down to the bone in minutes.

Page 30

The awesome Amazon river flows like a snake through the South American rainforest. Here, a caiman and an anaconda swim along in search of prey while red-bellied piranhas hunt other fish in the shallows. On the bank, grazing capybaras have just noticed the danger nearby – a jaguar in the undergrowth.

4 a stealthy jaguar

5 a forest crab on a branch

6 a black caiman catching a fish

7 a giant catfish

8 red-bellied piranhas

The mighty Mekong flows through Vietnam.

Boats travel along the Mekong river, carrying people and goods.

Congo river, Central Africa

Giant water lilies float like huge saucers on the River Amazon in South America. The leaves have spaces filled with air that keep them upright.

Insects land here and slide down into the leaf.

Pitcher plants have a cup-shaped leaf with slippery insides for catching insects. The insects fall in and are digested (broken down) by juices.

The bottom of the cup contains digestive juices.

River of life

Rainforests are warm and wet all year round because they grow along the Equator. They are also very humid, or steamy, because there is a lot of water vapour (steam) in the air. Rainforest plants thrive in these conditions, and in turn provide plenty of food for animals.

a simple dugout canoe, powered by an outboard motor

Great rivers flow through the world's rainforests. They include South America's Amazon and Orinoco rivers, the Congo in Central Africa and the Mekong in southeast Asia. These waterways are important transport routes, as well as being habitats for rare and unique animals.

the Orinoco river, seen from the air

The bird's long beak reaches deep inside the flower.

Passion flowers are pollinated by hummingbirds. As the birds feed on nectar, they are dusted with pollen.

sword-billed hummingbird

a fast-flowing stream in the rainforest of eastern Brazil

Bromeliad plants have spiky leaves that form a bucket shape and fill up with rain. Tadpoles use these as nursery ponds.

What is this?

1 Women cook meals over a fire.

2 The people sleep in hammocks.

3 The yano is made of wood and thatched palm leaves.

Page 18

Page 10

Amazon village

The Yanomami are people who live in the Amazon rainforest. They make clearings in the forest to build their villages. Each village is home to between 40 and 150 Yanomami people. They share a large, oval building, called a yano. Inside, each family has its own space.

The village is a busy place. Everyone has a job to do. Some people are helping to repair the yano. Others are cooking food for the day. Some are getting ready to go hunting in the forest, and some are tending the gardens at the edge of the clearing. In the middle of the village is an open space for playing and feasting.

Page 30

This is a close-up of flowers that a Yanomami child is wearing as an earring.

Rainforest living

People have lived in rainforests for thousands of years. They have learned which plants are good for food, medicine and building materials, and which animals to hunt for food. The forests give them all they need, so they treat them with respect.

The Dayak people of Borneo live in huge, wooden longhouses.

Dugout canoes are used as transport by many rainforest people. The Kuna people of Panama in Central America use canoes to travel between the islands they live on.

A dugout canoe is made from a rainforest tree trunk.

Huli warriors,
Papua New Guinea

Feathered headdresses and colourful costumes are worn by rainforest people for festivals. People also paint their bodies and faces, and wear jewellery made from feathers, shells and beads.

The Baka people of West Africa make huts from leaves and branches.

A Mbuti hunter uses a slingshot to kill birds. The Mbuti live in the Ituri rainforest in Central Africa. Apart from hunting, they also gather fruit, roots and honey to eat.

Bows and arrows are used for hunting animals in the forest and for fishing. This man is fishing from a dugout canoe. His arrow is tipped with poison to kill or stun the fish.

This Yawalapiti man of South America is fishing.

What is this?

1 An orang-utan mother cradles her baby.

2 Trucks are loaded up with timber.

3 The gold mine is where rainforest once grew.

Page 23

Under threat

Imagine a world without rainforests. So much forest is being destroyed that there may be none left in 50 years' time. If this happens, rainforest people will lose their way of life and many animals will become extinct (die out forever). The loss will also be a disaster for the world's climate.

4 A small plane flies overhead.

5 The plantation grows one crop – palm oil trees.

6 At the refinery, the palms are processed for their oil.

27

4

3

5

6

Huge areas of rainforest like this one in Borneo have already gone. Some trees have been chopped down for their valuable timber. Others are burned to clear space for large farms called plantations or for gold mines and new roads. Orang-utans and other animals are left stranded, with nowhere to live or find food.

This is the camouflaged coat of a rare clouded leopard.

Rainforest threats

There are many reasons why rainforests are being destroyed. Rainforest products, such as timber and gold, are very valuable. But, if the rainforests disappear, so will other resources – including plants that could be used as medicines.

gold mine, Brazil

Thousands of miners are brought in to dig for gold.

Rainforest animals are collected and sold as pets.

Mining for gold and other precious metals is damaging the rainforest. Huge areas of forest are cleared to make space for the mines and roads. The chemicals used by the miners poison rivers and animals.

The Spix macaw may already be extinct in the wild.

Palm fruits are grown on plantations for their oil.

The rosy periwinkle from Madagascar is one of many medicinal rainforest plants. It is used to treat people with leukaemia (cancer of the blood).

The leaves of the rosy periwinkle are collected and used to make medicine.

These rainforest people are protesting against the destruction of their lands in the Amazon.

Brazil nuts are just one of many different nuts and fruits that are harvested from the rainforest. They grow in hard cases inside huge pods.

Brazil nuts in a pod

Rainforest people are trying to fight back to protect their homes. In some places, though, their traditional ways of life have already been wiped out.

Some rainforest plants, such as orchids, grow on the branches of canopy trees. They are called **epiphytes**, or 'air plants'. Their roots soak up water from the moist air.

orchids

Many tall rainforest trees only have shallow roots for soaking up nutrients from the top layer of soil. For extra stability, huge supports, called **buttress roots**, grow out of their trunks.

buttress root

Plants

pink-toed tarantula

Beautiful **butterflies** live in the world's rainforests. Birdwings, the world's largest butterflies, live in southeast Asia and Australia.

male blue birdwing

Tarantulas are the world's largest spiders, growing as large as dinner plates. They come out at night to hunt. Despite their size, they do not usually attack humans.

Minibeasts

In **Asia**, patches of rainforest are found in India and the southeast. Rainforests also grow along the northeast coast of Australia and on the island of New Guinea.

Asia

Australia

Rainforests grow in West and Central **Africa**, along the Equator. Small areas also survive on Madagascar, off the east coast of Africa.

Africa

World

Rainforests receive at least 2,000mm of rain a year. Rain falls almost every day. The average temperature in the rainforest is around 25°C all year round.

Rainforest people live in harmony with the forest. They may clear small areas to live in, but after a few years, they move on and the trees can grow back.

Huli man, Papua New Guinea

Environment

More to explore

Rainforest trees, such as teak and mahogany, produce valuable timber. About half of the world's rainforests are being chopped down to make furniture and other products.

In their gardens, the Yanomami grow a **crop** called manioc, which looks like a long potato. This root vegetable is peeled, grated and made into flat loaves.

Yanomami woman preparing manioc

Millipedes like damp, dark places near the riverbank or on the forest floor. They crawl and climb slowly on their many legs, feeding on dead leaves and plants.

When food is short, **African driver ants** leave their nests in their millions and march across the forest floor. They are fearsome predators with powerful jaws.

The largest rainforest on Earth grows along the banks of the Amazon river in **South America**. It is about the same size as Australia.

South America

Explorers and adventurers map rainforest regions. In 2010 Ed Stafford became the first person to walk the whole length of the Amazon river.

the Amazon river

Trees and plants soak up carbon dioxide, a gas in the air that causes **global warming**. When rainforest is cut down, there is more carbon dioxide – and more global warming.

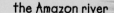

Rainforest rains drain into huge **rivers**. The Amazon is the largest of them all. It also has thousands of tributaries (streams that flow into it).

Index